Cowboys on the Western Trail

The Cattle Drive Adventures
of Josh McNabb and Davy Bartlett

ERIC OATMAN

PICTURE CREDITS
Cover: Private collection; pages 1, 11, 12-13, 21, 22-23, 25, 26
Peter Newark's Western Americana; pages 2-3, 37 (bottom),
39 © David R. Stoecklein; pages 4-5 Arrowsmith Collection;
pages 6 (bottom left), 7, 18-19, 28-29, 29 (top), 36 (top and bottom),
38 The Granger Collection, NY; page 6 (middle) Peck Collection; page 6
(top right) Jackson Collection; pages 6 (bottom right), 9 Courtesy of the
Library of Congress; page 6 (top left and background) CORBIS; page 6
(frames) Photodisc/Getty Images; page 8 (left) Glenbow Archives
NA2212-1; page 8 (left) Martin Rogers/CORBIS; page 10 (top) Diehl
Collection; pages 10 (bottom), 14 (inset) North Wind Picture Archives;
page 14-15 Bettmann/CORBIS; pages 16, 32 Montana Historical
Society; pages 16-17 The Erwin E. Smith Collection of the Library of
Congress on deposit at the Amon Carter Museum, Fort Worth, TX; page
20 (bottom) Kevin Morris/CORBIS; page 20 (top) Denver Public Library
Western Photograph Collection; pages 24-25 Courtesy of Brown and
Bigelow; pages 27, 30-31 Kansas State Historical Society, Topeka;
page 33 Ellwood House Museum; pages 34-35 Western History
Collection, University of Oklahoma Library; page 37 (top) Neill
Collection; page 40 Stockyard.

Library of Congress Cataloging-in-Publication Data

Oatman, Eric F.
   Cowboys on the Western trail : the cattle drive adventures of Joshua
McNabb and Davy Bartlett / by Eric Oatman.
     p. cm.
Summary: Recounts events of an 1877 cattle drive from southern
Texas to Ogallala, Nebraska, through the letters and journals of two
boys and an older member of the crew.
  ISBN 0-7922-6553-X
  [1. Cattle drives--West (U.S.)--Fiction. 2. Cowboys--West
(U.S.)--Fiction. 3. Frontier and pioneer life--West (U.S.)--Fiction. 4.
West (U.S.)--History--Fiction. 5. Diaries--Fiction. 6.
Letters--Fiction.] I. Title.
  PZ7.O1058Co 2004
  [Fic]--dc21
                           2003009164

Produced through the worldwide resources of the National Geographic
Society, John M. Fahey, Jr., President and Chief Executive Officer;
Gilbert M. Grosvenor, Chairman of the Board; Nina D. Hoffman,
Executive Vice President and President, Books and Education
Publishing; Ericka Markman, President, Children's Books and Education
Publishing Group; Steve Mico, Vice President Education Publishing
Group, Editorial Director; Marianne Hiland, Editorial Manager; Anita
Schwartz, Project Editor; Tara Peterson, Editorial Assistant; Jim Hiscott,
Design Manager; Linda McKnight, Art Director; Diana Bourdrez, Anne
Whittle, Photo Research; Matt Wascavage, Manager of Publishing
Services; Sean Philpotts, Production Coordinator; Jane Ponton,
Production Artist; Susan Donnelly, Children's Books Project Editor.

Production: Clifton M. Brown III, Manufacturing and Quality Control

PROGRAM DEVELOPMENT
Gare Thompson Associates, Inc.

BOOK DESIGN
Herman Adler Design

Published by the National Geographic Society
1145 17th Street, N.W.
Washington, D.C. 20036-4688

Printed in Spain

Table of Contents

North from Texas

From 1866 to 1886, cowboys herded, or drove, more than six million cattle north from Texas to the railroads in Missouri and Kansas. These cattle drives were full of adventure and excitement. Every spring and summer, Texas cowboys drove more than 200,000 cattle north. They sold the cattle in railroad towns with names like Abilene and Dodge City.

The U.S. Army bought some of the cattle to feed Native Americans in the Indian Territory (Oklahoma), Kansas, and Nebraska. Northerners just starting ranches also bought some. But trains shipped most of the cattle to slaughterhouses in Kansas City and Chicago. It seemed as if everyone in the country ate beef.

The cattle trade made money for the sellers. In 1865, Texans had six million head of cattle. In Texas, ranchers got about four dollars a head. In northern states they could get almost forty dollars a head. Ranchers and cowboys earned more money from selling cattle than they had thought possible.

The success of the cattle drives rested on the bravery of thousands of cowboys, or "cowpunchers," as they liked to be called. From 1866 to 1886, about 35,000 men drove cattle along the trails from Texas. Most of them were in their late teens or twenties. Half of them were African Americans or **Tejanos** (tay-HAH-nohs), Texans of Mexican descent. Many of the leaders of the drives were **vaqueros** (vah-KAIR-ohz), Mexican cowboys. Women did not travel on the cattle drives. They worked on ranches, herding cattle and helping to prepare for the long, hard drives.

WYOMING TERRITORY

DAKOTA TERRITORY

NEBRASKA

Ogallala

South Platte River

Ellsworth   Abilene

Dodge City   KANSAS

Arkansas River

COLORADO

Cimarron River

NEW MEXICO TERRITORY

Red River

INDIAN TERRITORY

Fort Griffin

Colorado River

Brazos River

TEXAS

San Antonio

N
W   E
S

WESTERN TRAIL
CHISHOLM TRAIL

MILES
0   100   200   300   400

0   100   200   300   400   500   600
KILOMETERS

MEET THE TRAIL CREW

In 1877, Josh McNabb, a **wrangler,** and Davy Bartlett helped 13 men drive 3,000 cattle from southern Texas to Ogallala, Nebraska. The 800-mile-trip took three months.

The boys and an older member of the crew tell the story of the drive in journals and letters. The crew members are fictional, but their stories are like those of many cowboys in the 1870s.

Josh McNabb, 14, wrangler

Davy Bartlett, 13, wagon driver

Duke Watson, 22, cowboy

Pedro Sanchez, 33, trail boss

Jack "Grub" Anson, 39, cook

CHAPTER 1

Spring Roundup

Cowboys began preparing for cattle drives in early April. Thousands of cattle had to be herded together, or rounded up. Ranches usually banded together to make roundups easier. Up to 20 ranches might be involved.

Ranchers sent 200 to 300 cowhands to a central camp. The cowhands worked day and night to bring in the cattle. They counted them and **branded** the new calves with their ranch's mark. Cowhands worked hard, but they also had fun. They played cards, had roping contests, and played jokes on one another. At night, they sang songs or told stories around the campfire. At daybreak, however, the work began and continued until nightfall.

Ranchers owned thousands of longhorn cattle. **Longhorns** were huge, half-wild animals. They could weigh up to 1,600 pounds. Their horns stretched four to six feet from tip to tip. Two features made them ideal for long trail rides. They could go without food or water for long periods, and their hooves were hard as rocks.

The Bartlett ranch, where our story begins, covers 20 square miles of hilly rangeland. Everyone on the ranch works the roundup, including the whole Bartlett family. Bartlett ranch cowboy Duke Watson leads the roundup.

April 10, 1877
Bartlett Ranch

Dear Brother and Sister,

This year, we're taking the herd north to Ogallala, Nebraska. Mr. Bartlett is paying an outfit from the Double X ranch to drive our herd of 2,000 and theirs of 1,000. My job will be to make sure they handle our cows well. They're sending a trail boss, a wrangler, a cook, and 10 hands. The wrangler, Josh McNabb, is a boy of 14. He is in charge of a group of 80 horses—8 for each man. Mr. Bartlett will meet us in Ogallala to sell the cows and pay the crew.

Davy, Bartlett's son, is turning out to be a fine cowboy. He works hard all day without a complaint. He's been begging to go on the drive, but I don't know that the trail boss will want him along. Too bad, because I think he would do fine. He's tough. As we say, he's got "gravel in the gizzard." Work calls. We'll mail letters from the towns and forts along the trail.

Your loving brother,
Duke

Calves are branded with a hot iron.

April 12, 1877
Bartlett Ranch

Dear Mama,

    Here at the BR, the men have been branding calves for three days. Three more days, and we'll be on the trail again. Papa says I'm good with the horses. At night, I hobble them. That means I tie ropes around the front legs of the horses that won't settle down. That way, they won't run off.

    The hands have eight horses each. Every morning they pick out the one they want to start the day with. They save their best horses for night duty. Papa and I sure miss you. And the food—well, I wish it was yours. I miss your biscuits. Grub's our cook. The men say that Grub is the best trail cook anywhere.

Your son,

Joshua

from Davy Bartlett's journal
April 13, 1877

I helped Dad's men brand cows all day today. And I met a boy my age. His name is Josh McNabb. He is the wrangler in charge of the horses. His father is the crew's *segundo,* or second in charge. Josh sure is lucky. Josh said his father taught him to break in wild horses when he was nine. Duke says there is nothing more dangerous than breaking in a wild horse that has been running free all its life. He says nothing scares Josh. Wish they'd say that about me. I'd give anything to go on the trail. Duke tells me next year for sure. A year is *too* long to wait!

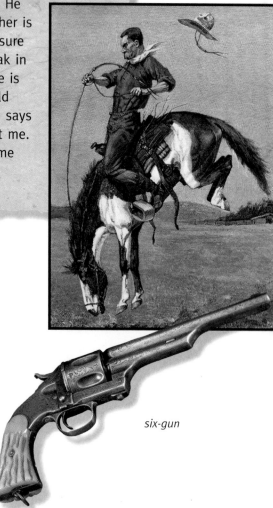

six-gun

Cowboys were a special breed. The good ones were called "stayers." Day and night, they stayed with the herd no matter what. They weren't complainers. They put up with blistering sun, drenching rain, dust, thirst, hunger, lack of sleep, and **stampedes**. They all carried six-guns, more for show than anything else. But they weren't afraid to use all six bullets when thieves tried to steal their cattle and horses. And they stood up to Indians who didn't want them to cross their land.

The cowboys worked hard for about a dollar a day. That was good money. They paid for their clothes and equipment, but otherwise they lived off the ranch.

Accepting meals at different ranches was called "riding the grub line." They lived in bunkhouses that were cold in winter and hot in summer. They didn't wash often. They worked hard, and most loved their jobs.

CHAPTER 2

Cowmen on the Trail

All the cowboys listened to the trail boss. The trail boss was tough, but fair. He had to be able to make fast decisions and recognize trouble and how to avoid it. He looked for men who had top roping and riding skills. He turned down those who angered easily, thought too highly of themselves, or seemed lazy. He didn't hire men who took too little care of their horses or too many risks around longhorns.

Some cattle drives used the Shawnee Trail. Others used the Chisholm Trail. In 1876, cowmen started to use another route, the Western Trail. The trail went north through Texas, crossed the Indian Territory and Kansas, and ended up at Ogallala, Nebraska. The Bartlett trail boss, Pedro Sanchez, and his crew would take the Western Trail.

from Davy Bartlett's journal
April 14, 1877

I'm going on the drive! Here's how it happened. I was helping to brand the cows when the trail boss walked over. He told me the old wagon driver was going to quit. He asked me if I could drive a supply wagon. I told him I sure could. Then we went to talk to Pa. Pa said he guessed I was old enough. Next thing I knew, the old wagon driver, Pokey, was showing me how to pack supplies into a wagon. We hitched up the mules and let them pull us around the bunkhouse for practice. We stopped, and he got off. "You'll do fine," he said. I'm nervous but real proud.

April 14
Bartlett Ranch

Dear Mama,

   We are pulling out tomorrow. When I watch the men work the longhorns, I'm glad I only deal with horses. Duke keeps saying that longhorns have "cow sense," and I guess he's right. Yesterday, thunder rolled through. The cattle quickly got together. Seems like they can sense danger. They made a circle around the calves. Luckily, we didn't have a storm. That might have made 'em stampede. One cowboy told me to stay away from the bulls. He said they are meaner than buffalo or a grizzly bear. I do not plan on going near the bulls!

   Mr. Sanchez is a tough boss. He just looks at the men, and they jump to work. But he seems fair too.

   Guess what? Another boy, named Davy, is going on the drive with us. He's the owner's son. I wonder if we will be friends.

Your son,
Joshua

13

A herd of 3,000 cattle is huge and hard to control. But the trail boss and his crew were used to large herds.

The herd made a cloud of dust that could be seen from miles away. The cattle didn't move in a single line. They moved two, three, four, or more abreast. They lumbered along at two miles an hour. Cowboys rode in front, back, and on both sides of the cattle. They kept them moving forward. It could take hours to get the cattle off the ranch and onto the trail.

CHAPTER 3

Moving Out

Herds usually moved 10 or 15 miles a day. But the first day was always different. If the cattle were only 12 miles from home, they might turn around and start back. Often, the trail boss pushed the cattle hard. This meant the men worked from seven in the morning until late that first night.

The cowboys took turns watching the cattle all night. Three men worked each shift on their "night horses"—the most sharp-eyed and surefooted ones. To keep the cattle calm, the men sang. Some sang hymns. Others sang songs they had just made up or learned years before.

from Josh McNabb's journal

April 15, 1877

I hardly see Pa. He rides in front of the herd. By the time I see him at night, we're both too tired to talk. I helped Davy gather wood when we stopped to rest. We loaded it under a wagon in the "possum pouch." This is a blanket stretched under a wagon. The horses are fine so far. But it sure is hot on the trail. After an hour, my shirt sticks to me. I use the hat Ma bought me all the time. Five dollars seemed a lot for the hat at the time, but it keeps me cool. Davy wishes he had one. At night it's so cold, I try to sleep near the fire.

April 22

All I want to do is sleep. I miss my soft bed. We have been on the trail for seven days now, most of the time in hill country. The longhorns are powerful critters, but the climbing has been hard on them. The horses get tired too. The men sometimes go through more than three horses a day. Soon we'll be on the range. No more hills, just flat land. I'll miss the hills.

We gathered some cow chips for fires. Wood is hard to find. The food is getting better. Grub makes good hot bread and coffee. But his specialty is son-of-a-gun stew. It tastes different every time. He throws whatever he has handy into a pot of beans and cooks it up, so it's always a surprise. Mostly it's different meats, tongue, and any part of the cow he has. He also adds skunk eggs. That's what he calls onions!

from Davy Bartlett's journal
May 2, 1877

We crossed to the east side of the Colorado River today. It was a pretty easy crossing. The river was shallow where we crossed. Josh led his horses over first, and the cattle followed. The mules had no trouble pulling the wagons across. Still, everyone is tired, so we are going to lay over for a day. I'll finally be able to wash up, the first time in two weeks.

The thing that bothers me the most are the blow flies. There seem to be millions of them. They can kill the cattle if they get into a longhorn's open wounds. Duke spotted one longhorn that had swollen ears. He quickly opened the area with his knife, scooped out the worms, and doused the wound with carbolic acid and axle grease. That should cure it!

from Josh McNabb's journal
May 3, 1877

Davy and I were talking about Mr. Sanchez. He is amazing. He never seems tired. He is like an Indian scout, riding 10 miles ahead of the herd. He looks for trouble, like buffaloes or another herd. He chooses places to rest the herd at noon and at night. Then he hurries back to tell Grub and me the spots he has chosen. Our wagons move much faster than the cattle. By the time the herd reaches us, we have lunch or supper ready.

The men respect Mr. Sanchez. Grub says the men think highly of all vaqueros, though they would never say so. Duke agrees. After all, there were vaqueros 200 years before us cowboys. We even use some words from their language. Our word "ranch" comes from their *rancho*. Vaqueros call their roundups *rodeos*. They protect their legs with leather leggings called *chaparreras*. We protect ours with chaps. They taught us how to tame wild horses called *mesteños*. We call those horses "mustangs." We keep them in small herds we call "remudas," just like the Mexicans do. No wonder Mr. Sanchez is such a good trail boss. His ancestors *invented* cowboys.

from Davy Bartlett's journal
May 10, 1877

Tomorrow, I'll be at Fort Griffin. Settlers go to the store there to sell eggs, milk, butter, and fresh beef to the horse troops. They also sell them to the storeowner. I'll stay with the mules while Mr. Sanchez and Grub pick up supplies. A company of buffalo soldiers is posted there! They're famous! Every soldier in the regiment is a black man. Duke once told me about them. "They're the best Indian fighters in the West," he said. He asked one soldier if he'd ever fought an Indian. "We protect settlers and mail coaches," is all he said. "That's our job."

A buffalo soldier

The next stop on the trail was Buffalo Gap. For centuries, buffalo herds had traveled through this natural cut in the hills. They were on their way to grazing land in the north. Now buffalo hunters made their winter camp here. At Fort Griffin nearby, they sold the animals they shot.

The storeowner at the post bought the carcasses for 5 to 15 dollars each. He sold the meat to the soldiers and local settlers.

His partner took the hides and bones to Dodge City, where they fetched a lot of money. Traders bought the bones by the ton and shipped them to the East. The bones were used to make fertilizer, china, and buttons.

After leaving the hills, the cattle marched through rainbows of wild flowers to Fort Griffin. Its whitewashed stone buildings stood high on a hill. The men didn't let the cattle stop until they had crossed the shallow Clear Fork of the Brazos River.

CHAPTER 4

Dangers on the Trail

The biggest fear of the cowboys on the trail was a stampede. Storms often caused stampedes. Dark clouds usually meant trouble.

There were two ways to stop a stampede: let the cattle run until they were tired out, or make them mill. To make them mill, the cowboys had to turn the leaders sharply to the right. The other longhorns would follow, moving clockwise. When the cattle were trapped in the center of the milling beasts, the stampede would be over.

When the night sky filled with dark clouds, Sanchez made the men mount up. They were getting ready for the worst—3,000 stampeding cattle. Tired animals were less likely to run than rested ones, but these longhorns had been resting all day. By dusk, sheets of water were falling. Then it happened. A thunderbolt split the sky. The longhorns were off! Sanchez decided to mill the herd.

from Josh McNabb's journal
May 16, 1877

I was scared during that stampede! It all happened so fast. Luckily, Papa's horse knew what to do. It slammed its body against the lead steer, pushing the three-quarter-ton beast to the right. Caught between the two animals, Papa's leg was hurt.

Sanchez pushed his horse past Papa and around the steer's horns. He whirled his poncho round and round above his head, and shouted in Spanish. The steer looked up at the spinning poncho and turned. The herd followed the leader into an ever-tightening circle. In 15 minutes, the milling stopped. The stampede was over.

from Davy Bartlett's journal
May 18, 1877

That stampede was sure exciting, even though I almost got killed. I was standing next to the chuck wagon—the wagon with the stove and food. The cows started to run. I tried to push the wagon out of the way, but it wouldn't budge without the mules to pull it. One of the cowboys saved it. "Get out of the way!" he yelled. He tossed his rope over the wagon seat like it was a longhorn. Then he wrapped his end of the rope around his saddle horn. His horse dug its hooves into the ground and backed up, pulling the wagon with it.

By now, the men had been on the Western Trail for a long time. They were hot and tired. They knew that they had to cross the Red River. Crossing the Red River could be dangerous. Graves bordering the river proved that. The men prepared to herd the cattle slowly through the red waters and up the red bluff banks.

The herd crossed the Red River slowly. The men urged the reluctant cattle on. If one cow slipped and fell, it would throw the whole herd off. So, the men talked to the animals as they led them to the other side. The wagons got stuck in the mud, but the men managed to pull them out. Everyone wanted to rest, but they herded for three more hours. Then the **outfit** was in Indian Territory.

They would stay in Indian Territory for 200 miles. The Indian Territory (later Oklahoma) was land the U.S. government had set aside for Indians who had been forced from their homelands. The Indians who lived there weren't happy about Texas herds crossing their lands. Sometimes they made cowboys pay a "tax" of several head of cattle. Other times they started a stampede. Then they gathered up any longhorns that strayed from the herd.

from Josh McNabb's journal
May 30, 1877
We met Quanah Parker. He looks like a fierce leader. He has led his Comanche braves in many battles. So far, no one has defeated him. He wanted to trade some items with us. We gave him whatever he asked for, and then he left. Pa says we are lucky he was in a peaceful mood.

Quanah Parker

June 1, 1877

I didn't know what the commotion was last night, but Duke and Mr. Sanchez did. Rustlers! Sanchez leaped on his horse and ordered me to follow him. About 10 minutes out, the three of us saw the shapes of horses running against the full moon. Someone had taken the hobbles off their legs.

Finally we caught up with three rustlers. Mr. Sanchez shot into the air and yelled, "Stop!" They stopped their horses and put their hands in the air. Their faces were painted, but they were wearing clothes any ranch hand would wear. They were white men disguised as Indians! We collected our horses—and took theirs too. Mr. Sanchez said we had no time to take them to jail.

Small groups of **rustlers,** or cattle thieves, were as big a threat to the cattle drive as Indians were. Cowboys never knew when these thieves would come. Rustlers were usually men, though some rustlers were women. One woman, known as Cattle Kate, was caught and hanged for her crimes in Wyoming.

On June 8, the cowmen drove the cattle into Kansas. They spent a day getting across the muddy Cimarron River and camped on the other side.

Cattle Kate

CHAPTER 5

The Queen of Cow Towns

The grass had been good in the Indian Territory. It was even better in Kansas. The longhorns had been putting on weight. This was a good thing, since they would be more valuable at Dodge City and Ogallala.

On June 12, they reached Dodge. The tracks of the Santa Fe Railroad had been laid as far as Dodge by 1872. By 1877, Dodge was the world's biggest cattle market—the Queen of Cow Towns, cowboys called it.

Although Dodge had wooden planks for sidewalks, it was like any other cow town. In summer, the place was a dust bowl. The town smelled of cows and dirty cowboys. The first things most cowboys did were to get a bath and buy new clothes. They threw out the old ones.

Sanchez had the men drive their cattle four miles to the Arkansas River. They set up camp for the night. In the morning, they separated the oldest cattle from the youngest. That left 1,400 head of cattle. These would be going into Dodge and then to meatpacking plants in Chicago.

Front Street, Dodge City, late 1800s

Dodge was known as a tough cow town. Saloon keepers and gamblers ran the town. Two lawmen kept order during the summer months. One of them was a police officer, Wyatt Earp. Earp sometimes had help from Bat Masterson, the county sheriff. When Davy got there, Earp was 29 years old. Masterson was 24.

from Davy Bartlett's journal
June 22, 1877
Mr. Sanchez is letting us go into town. We're going in four at a time. The others will watch the herd. After the rustlers, Mr. Sanchez is not taking any chances. He gave us an advance on our salaries of 20 dollars. That's our wages for almost 3 weeks. Josh and I promised each other we'd only spend 5 dollars in town. We'll save the rest. Maybe I'll meet Wyatt Earp!

Wyatt Earp

from Josh McNabb's journal
June 22, 1877

We all had our hair trimmed. Then Pa said we'd stay in a hotel. Even I want a bath. Cowboys fill the streets. Pa says to watch our backs. The town is dangerous. Even if Wyatt Earp is a lawman, sometimes cowboys just like to pick a fight with him. Duke picked up a newspaper to read. Funny, I never think of Duke reading, but he says he loves to read. He writes songs too.

While Pa and Duke went in to get us a room, Wyatt Earp came out. He pulled his handlebar mustache and tipped his hat. Davy and I were so surprised to see him, we couldn't say a word!

Cowboys drive longhorns through Dodge City.

June 23, 1877
Dodge City

Dear Mama,
    Yesterday, Duke, Papa, Davy, and I were watering our horses outside a saloon. Two men with metal stars on their shirts strolled out. One was Wyatt Earp. The other was Bat Masterson. Everyone on the street looked up when they walked out.
    Then we heard gunshots coming from the street. Earp and Masterson broke into a run. Davy and I stared. A cowboy was shooting his six-gun into the air. Everyone froze. Masterson walked up behind him, grabbed the man's gun, and took the bullets out. He handed the gun back to the cowboy. "Do that again," Masterson said, "and we'll shoot you with it." Then, as if nothing had happened, everything went back to the way it was. Davy loves it here, but I like it better on the trail.

Your son,
Joshua

P.S. Papa's leg is much better!

from Davy Bartlett's journal
June 24, 1877

We ate a big dinner at a hotel. Then we rented a room there for the night for 3 dollars. It was kind of dirty, but Josh and I didn't care. It was fun to sleep in a hotel.

For 50 cents we could have a bath in a tub on the first floor. We all used the same water to save money. Josh went first, then me. Mr. McNabb and Duke flipped a coin to see who would go next. Mr. McNabb won. By the time Duke got in, the water was kind of a rusty black. He just laughed and took his bath anyway.

Up in the room, the men gave us the bed. They bunked on the floor. But Josh and I couldn't get to sleep. After an hour, we figured out why. We weren't used to soft beds anymore. So, we got down on the floor. In a minute, we were sound asleep.

Dodge City, Kansas, 1876

After breakfast, the four walked down to the cattle pens and watched a herd of cattle being loaded onto a train. They saw Sanchez talking to a cattle trader. The trader gave Sanchez a piece of paper. It was a bank draft. A bank draft is a written order telling a banker to pay money from a bank account. Bank drafts were used instead of actual cash. It was time to turn over half the herd. The longhorns were sold for far more than they would have brought in Texas.

Cowboys use long prods to force cattle up a chute and into a railroad car.

CHAPTER 6

The End of the Trail

Ogallala was three weeks away from Dodge. It was a long, hot trip over a flat, almost treeless plain. The outfit entered Nebraska on July 12 with the remaining 1,600 cattle. They had 75 miles to go. Men who had taken this route before knew what was ahead. There would be searing sun, hot winds, and little water. The last day's drive was the worst. It was 30 waterless miles from the head of Stinking Water Creek to the South Platte River and Ogallala. Along the way, the men saw a sight that put dread in their hearts. Barbed wire fenced in much of the land and the cattle. The open spaces seemed slowly to be disappearing.

The men drove the herd hard all day. By mid-afternoon, the tongues of the horses and cattle hung out of their mouths. Just before dusk, the men saw the black smoke of a Union Pacific train.

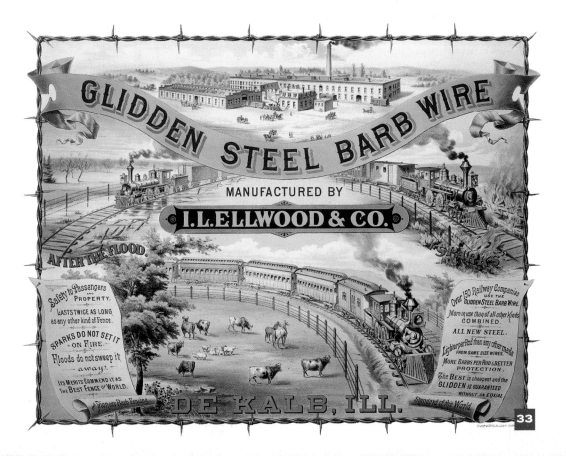

from Davy Bartlett's journal

July 13, 1877

Pa's been in Ogallala arranging for the rest of the herd to be sold. When he heard we were camped on the South Platte, he came out from town to meet us. He and Mr. Sanchez had a long talk by the fire. They agreed to meet in town in the morning. Pa didn't even ask me if I wanted to go back to the ranch with him. He knew I couldn't go. I've traveled with this outfit almost 1,000 miles. I'm not going to let them down now.

July 13, 1877
Nebraska

Dear Mama,

   Last night I saw the strangest sight of my life. A kind of blue light came down from somewhere and settled over everything. Davy and I saw it together. For a time we thought the cows' horns were on fire. Then the light disappeared, and the longhorns ran. The men just let them tire themselves out. In the morning I asked Papa about the light. "That was Saint Elmo's fire," he said. "I've only seen it once before. It usually happens just before or after a thunderstorm. Maybe a scientist can explain it. I can't." Maybe I'll find out the answer sometime. I like riding the trail, but nature interests me more. I guess I'm like you. I want answers to my questions.

                                   Your son,
                                   Joshua

July 17, 1877
Near Ogallala

Dear Mama,

This time we didn't have to wait our turn for the cattle pens. These longhorns aren't going to Chicago. They're going north about 30 miles. They will stock a ranch started just this year. The rancher signed for 600 head from the Double X and 1,000 head from Bartlett's. He came to our camp with his men. He was a tall man, maybe 31 years old, with a pointed beard. It was Buffalo Bill Cody! We could hardly believe it. He told us about being a pony express rider when he was our age. He said he loved danger too.

I wanted to say something clever. All I could think to say was, "Why do they call you Buffalo Bill, sir?" He just smiled, so Papa answered for him. "About 10 years ago, Mr. Cody got a contract to supply buffalo meat for the men building the Union Pacific Railway. He killed more than 4,000 buffalo all by himself."

Mr. Cody and his crew bought 1,600 head of cattle, all but a few of our horses, the supply wagon, and even Grub's chuck wagon. Hooray! Now we are off to see Ogallala!

Your son,
Joshua

A pony express rider delivering mail

Buffalo Bill

from Davy Bartlett's journal
July 19, 1877
Yesterday morning, we all packed up our gear and rode into town. Ogallala is like Dodge—dirty and dusty and rowdy. It's got cattle pens and loading chutes and cattlemen buying and selling steers. All this is in a place that's hardly more than a block long. Railroad Street is where everything happens. Josh and I found a clothing store there. We looked at hats and boots, but we didn't buy anything. Later, we all met for lunch. We ate like we hadn't seen food in months. I can't believe the ride is over.

July 23, 1877
Ogallala

Dear Brother and Sister,
    Our trail drive has ended. It was a complete success. Before the drive, I told you that I feared the crew would be shorthanded. It was not, thanks to a trail boss who is an excellent judge of men and an even better leader. The boy of 14 whom I mentioned in my last letter proved to be one of the best wranglers I have ever known. The 13-year-old son of my employer at the Bartlett Ranch served as a supply wagon driver. We were all proud of both of them.
    I hurt my hand during a stampede, but it is better. Trailing punishes the body, but I love the wide-open prairie here. It refreshes my spirit. That is why I will stay in Texas.

Your loving brother,
Duke

Epilogue

John Rufus Blocker is the man who led the last cattle drive on the Western Trail in 1893. He went to Deadwood, South Dakota. By then, three to five million cattle had passed along the trail. Many things ended the cattle drives. The invention of barbed wire stopped the cattle from freely roaming the trails. A cattle disease called Texas fever killed many cattle and caused the longhorn to be banned from many northern states. But ranching and cowboys remained a big part of the West.

Davy worked on the Bartlett ranch year round. After his father died, Davy joined a rodeo, roping steers and riding broncos. Josh went to college and learned how to improve cattle. Josh and Davy remained friends. Each year, their families got together. Each gathering began with one of them saying, "Why, you remember, when. . . ."

Glossary

brand–to burn a mark that identifies a cow's owner on the skin with a hot iron

longhorns–a breed of cattle with long horns common in Southwestern United States

outfit–a team of ranch hands

rustlers–cattle or horse thieves

stampede–a sudden rush of frightened animals

Tejano–a Texan whose ancestors came from Mexico

vaquero–a cowboy or ranch hand

wrangler–a cowboy who takes care of saddle horses 4100077